THE VIKINGS

300 QUOTES, SAYINGS AND FACTS ABOUT THE NORSE WARRIORS OF ANCIENT SCANDINAVIA

Mick Kremling

"I CAME INTO THIS WORLD KICKING AND SCREAMING, COVERED IN ANOTHER'S BLOOD. I INTEND TO GO OUT OF THIS WORLD IN THE SAME WAY."

-UNKNOWN VIKING WARRIOR

"THE LAME MAN RUNS IF HE HAS TO."

-OLD NORDIC PROVERB

3

"EVERY MAN IS MASTER OF HIS OWN WORDS."

-THE SAGA OF GRETTIR

4

"THE HAVAMAL" IS A COLLECTION OF OLD NORSE POEMS AND STORIES FROM THE VIKING AGE.

"HE IS TRULY WISE WHO'S TRAVELLED FAR AND KNOWS THE WAYS OF THE WORLD. HE WHO HAS TRAVELLED CAN TELL WHAT SPIRIT LEADS THE MEN THAT HE MEETS."

-THE HAVAMAL

"CATTLE DIE. KINSMEN DIE.
ALL MEN ARE MORTAL.
WORDS OF PRAISE WILL
NEVER PERISH NOR A
NOBLE NAME."

-THE HAVAMAL

"FLATTERY LOOKS LIKE FRIENDSHIP, AS THE WOLF LOOKS LIKE THE DOG."

-NORDIC PROVERB

"THE SUMMER MOMENTS ALWAYS PASS QUICKLY."

-NORSE PROVERB

THE VIKINGS WERE THE ANCIENT PEOPLES WHO INHABITED SCANDINAVIA FROM THE LATE 8TH CENTURY TO THE EARLY 11TH CENTURY A.D. THEY WOULD EVENTUALLY SETTLE GREENLAND, ICELAND, AND EVEN PARTS OF NORTH AMERICA FOR A TIME.

ON JUNE 8TH, 793 A.D.
SEVERAL NORSE SHIPS
LANDED ON THE ISLAND OF
LINDISFARNE, JUST EAST
OF ENGLAND. THE
NORSEMEN LOOTED AND
BURNT A CATHOLIC
CHURCH THERE, AND
KILLED MANY IT'S THE
MONKS. THIS EVENT
MARKED THE BEGINNING
OF THE VIKING AGE.

11

"WHEN ILL SEED HAS BEEN SOWN, SO TOO, ILL THE CROP WILL BE."

-THE SAGA OF NJAL

"A KING'S SON SHOULD BE THOUGHTFUL, THOROUGH, AND SILENT BRAVE IN BATTLE. A MAN SHOULD BE HAPPY AND IN GOOD HUMOR TO HIS DYING DAY."

-THE HAVAMAL

WHEN A VIKING DIED IN
BATTLE, HE WAS BELIEVED
TO ASCEND TO VALHALLA.
VALHALLA WAS THE
NORSE HEAVEN, IN WHICH
THE DEAD FEASTED AT
LONG TABLES. THERE
WOULD BE FIGHTING,
WOMEN, AND DRINKING
FROM THE SKULLS OF
THEIR ENEMIES.

"IT IS BETTER TO STAND AND FIGHT. IF YOU RUN, YOU WILL ONLY DIE TIRED."

-VIKING PROVERB

"DO NOT WEEP MOTHER, IF WE ARE KILLED IT WILL BE SAID OF YOU THAT YOU HAD GOOD SONS."

-GRETTIR

THE WORD "VIKING" IN OLD NORSE WORD "VIKINGR" MEANING "FROM THE SEA" OR "SEAFARER/TRAVELLER".

"LET ANOTHER'S WOUNDS BE YOUR WARNING."

-THE SAGA OF NJAL

"TELL NOT AN EVIL MAN WHAT MISFORTUNES BEFALL THEE."

-THE HAVAMAL

THE VIKINGS WERE EXPERT
SHIPBUILDERS. THEIR
ICONIC "LONGSHIPS" WERE
LONG AND SLENDER,
COULD BE SAILED IN
SHALLOW WATER, AND
COULD EASILY BE PULLED
ON AND OFF BEACHES. THE
SHIPS WERE DESIGNED FOR
LIGHTNING FAST RAIDS ON
TOWNS AND VILLAGES BY
THE COASTS.

"A COWARDLY MAN THINKS HE WILL LIVE FOREVER IF WARFARE HE AVOIDS, BUT OLD AGE WILL GIVE HIM NO PEACE, THOUGH SPEARS MAY SPARE HIM.

-THE HAVAMAL

"THE BEAUTIFUL WOMAN FINDS NOT THE COWARD'S BED."

-VIKING PROVERB

THE VIKINGS RELIGION
WAS OLD NORDIC
PAGANISM. THE NORSE
GODS WERE SEPARATED
INTO TWO GROUPS. THE
AESIR AND THE VANIR. IT
IS SAID A GREAT WAR WAS
WAGED BETWEEN THE TWO
GROUPS, RESULTING IN
BOTH GROUPS UNIFYING
INTO ONE SINGULAR
PANTHEON.

"HE FLEES NO FIRE, WHO JUMPS OVER IT."

-THE SAGA OF KING HROLFR KRAKI

"COURAGE IS BETTER THAN KEENEST STEEL."

-SIGURTH, FAFNISMAL

SOME THE MOST
PROMINENT AESIR GODS
INCLUDE:

ODIN, KING OF ALL THE
GODS.

THOR, THE THUNDER GOD
AND THE STRONGEST,

TYR, THE GOD OF WAR AND
SINGLE COMBAT.

"BRAWLS AND BICKERING I BRING THE GODS, THEIR ALE I SHALL MIX WITH EVIL."

-LOKI, THE GOD OF TRICKERY

"FOR HIM WHO SPEAKS
WITH THE HARD OF HEART,
WILL CHATTERING EVER
WORK ILL."

-ODIN, VAFPRUONISMAL

SOME OF THE MOST
PROMINENT VANIR GODS
INCLUDE:

SKADI, GODDESS OF
WINTER AND THE HUNT.

FREYJA, ASSOCIATED WITH
LOVE, BEAUTY AND
FERTILITY.

NJORD, ASSOCIATED WITH
WIND AND SEA.

"EVER WOULD ODIN WANDER ON THIS EARTH, WEIGHED WITH WISDOM AND FOREKNOWING, THE LORD OF LORDS AND LEAGUERED GODS, HIS SEED SOWING SIRE OF HEROES."

"MANY A FINE SKIN HIDES A FOUL MIND."

-EYRBYGGJA SAGA

"STRENGTH IS LIFE,

FOR THE STRONG HAVE THE RIGHT TO RULE."

"HONOR IS LIFE,

FOR WITHOUT HONOR ONE MAY AS WELL BE DEAD."

"LOYALTY IS LIFE,

FOR WITHOUT ONE'S CLAN

ONE HAS NO PURPOSE."

"DEATH IS LIFE,

ONE SHOULD DIE AS THEY HAVE LIVED."

IF A VIKING DIED OUTSIDE OF BATTLE, HE WOULD BE SENT TO HEL, A FREEZING COLD HALL THATS ROOF WAS MADE FROM THE SPINES OF SERPENTS THAT DRIPPED POISON ON THOSE BELOW. THERE WAS NO FEASTING AND THE DEAD COULD ONLY QUENCH THEIR THIRST WITH GOAT URINE.

"HEL'S HAIL IS CALLED ELJUDNIR, HER DISH IS HUNGER, HER KNIFE IS FAMINE."

-GYLFAGINNING

"A TRUE FRIEND WHOM
YOU TRUST WELL AND
WISH FOR HIS GOOD WILL;
GO TO HIM OFTEN,
EXCHANGE GIFTS, AND
KEEP HIM COMPANY."

-THE HAVAMAL

"A MAN IS NOT JUDGED BY THE MANNER IN WHICH HE LIVED, BUT BY THE MANNER IN WHICH HE DIED."

-NORDIC PROVERB

THE VIKING PEOPLE WERE
ORGANIZED INTO THREE
CLASSES:

THRALLS, THE SLAVES.

KARLS, THE FREE
PEASANTS.

JARLS, THE ARISTOCRACY.

"WITH LAW OUR LAND
WILL BE SETTLED, AND
WITH LAWLESSNESS
WASTED."

--THE SAGA OF NJAL

"EVERY MAN IS THE SMITH OF HIS OWN FORTUNE."

THE AVERAGE LIFE EXPECTANCY IN SCANDINAVIA DURING THE VIKING AGE WAS AROUND 45 YEARS OLD FOR ME. IT WAS ABOUT 10 YEARS LESS FOR WOMEN, WHO HAD TO ENDURE THE DANGERS OF CHILDBIRTH. THUS, IT WAS COMMON FOR AN OLDER MAN TO HAVE A MUCH YOUNGER WIFE.

ONLY ABOUT 80% OF
CHILDREN SURVIVED THE
FIRST FIVE YEARS OF LIFE
AND ONLY ABOUT 70%
MADE IT TO ADULTHOOD.

THE NORSE PEOPLE
VALUED STRENGTH AND
TOUGHNESS HIGHLY. IF A
VIKING CHILD WAS
DEEMED SICKLY,
DISFIGURED, OR TOO WEAK
TO CONTRIBUTE TO THE
FAMILY OR THEIR SOCIETY,
IT WOULD BE ABANDONED
OR THROWN INTO THE SEA
TO DROWN.

"WHAT IS HIDDEN IN SNOW,

IS REVEALED AT THAW."

HONOR WAS EXTREMELY IMPORTANT TO A VIKING. ATTACKS ON ONE'S PERSONAL HONOR, OR THAT OF HIS FAMILY OR HOMELAND WARRANTED IMMEDIATE RETALIATION. A MAN WAS EXPECTED TO RESPOND WITH VIOLENCE, EVEN IF IT MEANT DEATH FOR EITHER PARTY.

LOVE SONGS AND POEMS WERE OUTLAWED IN THE VIKING AGE. MEN FEARED MAGICAL ENSNAREMENT BY THE POWER FROM THE VERSES.

"MANY A MAN HAS BEEN BROUGHT TO DEATH BY OVERCONFIDENCE."

"MOST DEAR IS FIRE TO THE SONS OF MEN, MOST SWEET THE SIGHT OF THE SUN."

-THE HAVAMAL

/MANY VIKINGS WERE
INVOLVED IN THE
PROFITABLE SLAVE TRADE.
THESE SLAVES, OR
"THRALLS" AS THEY
CALLED THEM, WERE
YOUNG MEN AND WOMEN
TAKEN FROM SUCCESSFUL
RAIDS AND WOULD BE
SOLD AT SLAVE MARKETS
ACROSS EUROPE AND THE
MIDDLE EAST.

VIKING CHILDREN'S SOCIAL STATUS WAS DETERMINED BY THEIR PARENTS. IF A PARENT WAS A THRALL, THE CHILD WOULD BE A THRALL UNTIL ADULTHOOD.

THRALLS (VIKING SLAVES) HAD ABOUT THE SAME AMOUNT OF RIGHTS AS A FARM ANIMAL. DEPENDING ON THEIR OWNER, SLAVES WOULD BE BEATEN, SEXUALLY ABUSED, OR EVEN MURDERED OUTRIGHT WITH NO REPRISAL.

"THE SHAME YOU CANNOT LIFT AWAY, YOU HAD BETTER LET LIE."

-NORDIC PROVERB

"THERE ARE MORE THINGS
TO BE THOUGHT OF BY
MEN THAN MONEY ALONE."

-THE SAGA OF GRETTIR

ALTHOUGH FEARSOME WARRIORS AND RAIDERS, MOST VIKINGS LIVED AS FARMERS, MERCHANTS, INVENTORS, EXPLORERS AND MANY OTHER TYPICAL ROLES OF THE TIME PERIOD.

NOT MANY RECORDED BATTLES EXIST OF VIKINGS. THIS IS MAINLY DUE TO VIKINGS PREFERRING LIGHTNING FAST RAIDS RATHER THAN PITCHED BATTLES, ECONOMIC GAIN WAS THE VIKING RAIDERS MAIN PRIORITY, NOT CONQUEST.

"A TREE DOES NOT FALL AT THE FIRST BLOW."

-NORDIC PROVERB

"BETTER TO FIGHT AND FALL THAN TO LIVE WITHOUT HOPE"

-VOLSUNGA SAGA

THE MOST COMMON
WEAPON IN A VIKING
WARRIOR'S ARSENAL WAS
A SINGLE BLADED AXE.
THEY WERE MUCH EASIER
AND CHEAPER TO OBTAIN
THAN SWORDS.

SWORDS, BEING MUCH MORE EXPENSIVE TO FORGE AND HARDER TO OBTAIN, WOULD USUALLY BE CONSIDERED A FAMILY HEIRLOOM, GIVEN NAMES, AND PASSED DOWN FROM FATHER TO SON.

"WAKE EARLY IF YOU WANT ANOTHER MAN'S LIFE OR LAND. NO LAMB FOR THE LAZY WOLF, NO BATTLES WON IN BED."

-THE HAVAMAL

"NEVER WALK AWAY FROM HOME AHEAD OF YOUR AXE AND SWORD. YOU CAN'T FEEL A BATTLE IN YOUR BONES OR FORESEE A FIGHT."

-THE HAVAMAL

SOME VIKINGS HAD SWORDS MADE FROM "CRUCIBLE STEEL" THAT WAS NOT MADE AGAIN UNTIL THE INDUSTRIAL REVOLUTION, SOME 800 YEARS LATER. HOW THEY MADE THIS STEEL REMAINS A MYSTERY.

THE MOST COMMON TYPE OF SHIELD THE VIKINGS USED WAS THE ROUND SHIELD. THESE SHIELDS VARIED IN WOOD USED, BUT WERE TYPICALLY REINFORCED WITH LEATHER AND IRON AROUND THE RIM. THE SHIELDS WERE RATHER LARGE, MEASURING ABOUT 30" - 36".

VIKING ARMOR CONSISTED OF MANY VARIANTS OF RING MAIL AND CLOTH. TYPICALLY WEALTHIER OR MORE ACCOMPLISHED WARRIORS DONNED RING MAIL WHILST THE POORER VIKINGS MADE QUILTED CLOTH OR NO ARMOR AT ALL.

THE VIKINGS MADE USE OF
TWO KINDS OF KNIVES.

THE FIRST BEING THE "KNIFR"
THE PLAIN, SINGLE EDGED
KNIFE, NOT UNLIKE THOSE
USED BY OTHER CULTURES.

THE OTHER KNIFE, THE
"SEAX", WAS A HEAVIER TYPE
OF KNIFE SIMILAR TO THE
LIKENESS OF A MACHETE,
AND WAS ALMOST AS LONG
AS SOME SHORT SWORDS.

"THE BRAVE AND GENEROUS HAVE THE BEST LIVES. THEY ARE SELDOM SORRY. THE UNWISE MAN IS ALWAYS WORRIED, FEARING FAVORS TO REPAY."

-THE HAVAMAL

"FEAR NOT DEATH, FOR THE HOUR OF YOU DOOM IS SET AND NONE MAY ESCAPE IT."

SEVERAL OF THE VIKING SAGAS MENTION WARRIORS CALLED "BERSERKERS". THESE WARRIORS WERE SAID TO HAVE HAD MAGICAL POWERS WHICH RENDERED THEM IMMUNE TO HARM. IN ACTUALITY, THEY WOULD ENTER A TRANCE LIKE STATE, EITHER SOBER OR DRUGGED, AND FIGHT WILDLY AND OFTEN RECKLESSLY, CARING NOT AT ALL FOR THEIR OWN SAFETY.

"WOLF-SKINNED THEY ARE CALLED. IN BATTLE THEY BEAR BLOODY SHIELDS. RED ARE THEIR SPEARS WHEN THEY COME TO FIGHT"

"IF HAPLY I LEAD MY COMRADES OUT TO WAR, I SING 'NEATH THE SHIELDS, AND THEY MARCH FORTH SAFE INTO BATTLE, SAFE OUT OF BATTLE, AND SAFE RETURN FROM THE STRIFE."

--THE HAVAMAL

THE SPEAR WAS BY FAR
THE MOST COMMON
WEAPON USED BY THE
LOWER CLASSES IN VIKING
SOCIETY. THE WARRIOR
CLASS AND RAIDERS
WOULD MAKE USE OF
THEM AS THROWING
WEAPONS.

A HUSCARL, WERE THE HOUSEHOLD TROOPS OF A JARL, SIMILAR TO THAT OF A BODYGUARD, AND WERE USUALLY EQUIPPED WITH THE FINEST EQUIPMENT THE JARL COULD AFFORD (OR PLUNDER).

IN SOME CASES, VIKINGS
WERE KNOWN TO TAKE UP A
DEFENSIVE FORMATION
KNOWN AS A "SHIELD WALL"
IN WHICH EACH WARRIOR'S
SHIELD WOULD OVERLAP
WITH THEIR FELLOW
WARRIORS NEXT TO HIM,
PRESENTING AN
IMPENETRABLE LITERAL
WALL OF SHIELDS. IT WAS
SIMILAR TO THE GREEK
HOPLITE PHALANX
FORMATION.

"LET NO MAN SHOW GLORY
TOWARDS THE GREATNESS
OF HIS MIND; RATHER KEEP
WATCH OVER HIS WITS."

-NORDIC PROVERB

"LET US MAKE OUR DRAWN SWORDS GLITTER, YOU WHO STAIN THE WOLF'S TEETH WITH BLOOD; LET US PERFORM GREAT DEEDS."

VIKINGS WOULD OFTEN
WIELD LARGE TWO-
HANDED AXES. THESE
GREAT WEAPONS COULD
SPLIT SHIELDS AND
HELMETS WITH EASE,
THOUGH REQUIRED SPACE
TO WIELD EFFECTIVELY.

IT WAS COMMON FOR VIKINGS TO ATTACH METAL SPIKES OR STUDS, USUALLY OF IRON, TO THE CENTERS OF THEIR SHIELDS. THIS ALLOWED THEM TO USE THE SHIELD AS AN OFFENSIVE WEAPON.

"I RETURN YOUR AXE."

-THORGEIR TO THORFINN, AS HE SWUNG THE AXE, CHOPPING OFF HIS HEAD.

"IF YOU CANNOT BITE, NEVER SHOW YOUR TEETH."

THE VIKINGS WERE
UNUSUAL AND QUITE
UNIQUE IN THE FACT THEY
PUT MUCH PREFERENCE ON
THE USE OF AXE AND
GREAT AXE, AS THEIR
WEAPON OF CHOICE, AS
MOST EUROPEAN PEOPLES
AT THE TIME WERE KNOWN
FOR THEIR USE OF SPEAR,
SWORD, AND BOW.

VIKING WEAPONS WERE
INSCRIBED WITH RUNES,
WHICH WERE THOUGHT TO
GIVE THEM MAGICAL
POWERS OR BE BLESSED BY
A PARTICULAR GOD.

"OF HIS KNOWLEDGE A MAN SHOULD NEVER BOAST, RATHER HE MUST BE SPARING IN SPEECH WHEN TO HIS HOUSE THE WISER MAN COME. SELDOM DO THOSE WHO ARE SILENT MAKE MISTAKES. MOTHER WIT IS EVER A FAITHFUL FRIEND."

-THE HAVAMAL

"A CLEAVED HEAD NO LONGER PLOTS"

-NORDIC PROVERB

"WE WILL NEVER FLEE FROM OUR ENEMIES, WE WILL ENDURE THEIR WEAPONS."

--HJALMAR

"THE GODS HELP THOSE WHO HELP THEMSELVES."

DRAUGR IN NORSE MYTHOLOGY ARE BASICALLY ZOMBIES, WITH THEIR WITS STILL ABOUT THEM. THEY GUARD THEIR OWN GRAVES AND ANY TREASURE WITHIN FROM THIEVES AND TROUBLEMAKERS.

IN NORSE MYTHOLOGY,

SKOLL AND HATI

ARE THE NAMES OF THE
TWO WOLVES WHO
ENDLESSLY HUNT THE
MOON AND THE SUN.

"THE TWILIGHT OF THE GODS.
THERE WILL BE THREE YEARS
OF TERRIBLE WINTERS AND
SUMMERS OF BLACK
SUNLIGHT. MIDGARDSORMEN,
THE WORLD SERPENT, WILL
COME LUNGING FROM THE
OCEAN, DRAGGING THE TIDES
IN AND FLOODING THE
WORLD. THE WOLF GIANT,
FENRIR, WILL BREAK HIS
INVISIBLE CHAINS. THE SKIES
WILL OPEN AND SURT, THE
FIRE GIANT, WILL COME

FLAMING ACROSS THE BRIDGE
TO DESTROY THE GODS. ODIN
WILL RIDE OUT OF THE GATES
OF VALHALLA TO DO BATTLE
FOR THE LAST TIME AGAINST
FENRIR. THOR WILL KILL THE
SERPENT, BUT DIE FROM ITS
VENOM. SURT WILL SPREAD
FLAMES ACROSS THE EARTH,
AND AT LAST FENRIR WILL
SWALLOW THE SUN."

**-THE SEER, ON RAGNAROK,
BURIAL OF THE DEAD**

JORMUNGAND IS AN
ENORMOUS SEA SERPENT
WHO ENCIRCLES THE LAND
WHERE HUMANITY LIVES.
HE WILL FIGHT THOR, THE
THUNDER GOD, AT
RAGNAROK, THE ENDING
OF THE WORLD.

"THE WORLD WILL
SHUDDER WITH
EARTHQUAKES, AND
EVERY BOND AND FETTER
WILL BURST, FREEING
ODIN'S NEMESIS, THE
TERRIBLE WOLF FENRIR."

-RAGNAROK

ODIN, REFERED TO AS THE
ALL-FATHER, IS THE KING
OF THE GODS IN NORSE
MYTHOLOGY. HE IS THE
WISEST OF ALL THE GODS
AND IS DESCRIBED AS AN
ELDERLY MAN, WITH A
LONG BEARD AND ONE
EYE. A RAVEN IS OFTEN
DEPICTED ALONGSIDE HIM.

THE NINE WORLDS IN NORSE
MYTHOLOGY ARE:

ASGARD (HOME OF THE AESIR);
VANAHEIM (HOME OF THE
VANIR); ALFHEIM (HOME OF THE
ELVES); MIDGARD (EARTH);
JOTUNHEIM (HOME OF THE
GIANTS); SVALTALFHEIM (HOME
OF THE DWARFS); MUSPELHEIM
(HOME OF THE FIRE GIANTS);
NIFLHEIM (EMPTINESS AND A
POSSIBLE AFTERLIFE) AND HEL (A
GRIM PLACE FOR THE UNWORTHY
DEAD).

EINHERJAR IS THE NAME
FOR THE WARRIORS WHO
HAVE DIED IN BATTLE.
THEY ARE TAKEN TO
VALHALLA BY THE
VALKYRIES.

IN NORSE MYTHOLOGY,
VALKYRIES WERE SENT BY
ODIN TO EVERY BATTLE
WHERE THEY WOULD
CHOOSE WHICH MEN
WOULD DIE AND WHICH
WOULD HAVE VICTORY.

"FORTH SHALL WE FARE WHERE THE FRAY IS THICKEST, WHERE FRIENDS AND FELLOWS AGAINST FOEMEN BATTLE."

-THE SONG OF THE VALKYRIES

"START WE SWIFTLY WITH STEEDS UNSADDLED, HENCE TO BATTLE WITH BRANDISHED SWORDS!"

-THE SONG OF THE VALKYRIE, NJALS SAGA

THE GIANTS IN NORSE MYTHOLOGY REPRESENT DARKNESS, NIGHT, WINTER AND DEATH. THEY ARE THE ENEMIES OF THE GODS AND ARE KNOWN AS THE "DEVOURERS".

"OUT OF YMIR'S FLESH WAS FASHIONED OUT THE EARTH, THE SKY FROM THE FROST-COLD GIANT'S SKULL, AND THE OCEAN FROM HIS BLOOD."

-VAFPRUONISMAL

THE FANTASY CREATURES;
ELVES, DWARVES, TROLLS,
AND GIANTS, WERE FIRST
INTRODUCED IN NORSE
MYTHOLOGY. MODERN
INTERPRETATIONS ARE
LARGELY BASED ON NORSE
LORE.

IN NORSE MYTHOLOGY, THE DWARVES ARE MASTER CRAFTSMEN WHO LIVE UNDERGROUND. THE ELVES ARE BEAUTIFUL DEMIGOD LIKE BEINGS.

ASK AND EMBLA, ARE THE
FIRST TWO HUMANS
CREATED IN NORSE
MYTHOLOGY AND
REPRESENT MASCULINITY
AND FEMININITY.

THE VIKINGS HAD THREE
MAJOR FESTIVALS EACH
YEAR.

VETRARBLOT WAS IN
OCTOBER,

JOLABLOT IN JANUARY

AND SIGRBLOT IN APRIL.

"SHUN NOT THE MEAD, BUT DRINK IN MEASURE."

-THE HAVAMAL

"GIVE PRAISE TO THE DAY AT EVENING. TO A WEAPON THAT IS TRIED, TO A MAID AT WEDLOCK, TO ICE WHEN IT IS CROSSED, TO ALE WHEN IT IS DRUNK."

"COMES THE DARKNESS DRAGON, NITHHOGG, UPWARD FROM THE NITHA FELLS; HE BEARS IN HIS CLAWS NAKED CORPSES."

NIDHOGG IS A GIGANTIC DRAGON WHO CHEWS AT THE ROOTS OF YGGDRASIL, THE WORLD TREE. HE ALSO CHEWS ON THE CORPSES OF ALL THOSE WHO HAVE COMMITTED THE WORST OF CRIMES SUCH AS MURDER, RAPE AND TREACHERY,

IN THE EARLY VIKING AGE, THE NORSE USED RUNES OR "RUNOR" AS A SORT OF WRITTEN LANGUAGE BASED UPON SOUND VALUES, AMONGST THE PEOPLES OF SCANDINAVIA. CONTRARY TO POPULAR BELIEF, VIKINGS WERE NOT ILLITERATE AND COULD READ AND WRITE.

THERE IS EVIDENCE TO
SUGGEST THAT "RUNOR",
THE RUNIC ALPHABET OF
THE VIKINGS, WAS STILL IN
USE UP TO THE 15TH
CENTURY.

THE RUNIC ALPHABET "FUTHARK" COMES FROM THE VIKINGS AND CONSISTS OF 24 RUNES.

NORSE RUNES WERE THOUGHT TO HAVE COME FROM ODIN, WHEN HE SACRIFICED HIMSELF ON THE WORLD TREE, YGGDRASIL.

"A MAN SHOULD NOT CARVE RUNES, UNLESS HE KNOWS WELL HOW TO CONTROL THEM."

"VICTORY RUNES SHALL YOU KNOW, IF YOU WANT TO SECURE WISDOM, AND CUT THEM ON THY SWORD HILT, NAMING TYR, GOD OF WAR, TWICE."

MANY MODERN DAYS OF
THE WEEK ARE NAMED
AFTER NORSE GODS.
TUESDAY IS TYR'S DAY,
WEDNESDAY IS DERIVED
FROM ODIN (ALSO SPELLED
WODIN), THURSDAY IS
THOR'S DAY, AND FRIDAY
IS NAMED AFTER THE
GODDESS FREYA.

VIKING FAMILIES ALL
LIVED IN A SINGLE HOUSE.
EVERYONE FROM
CHILDREN, PARENTS, AND
GRANDPARENTS ALL HAD
CERTAIN DUTIES TO HELP
THE HOUSEHOLD RUN AND
PROSPER.

"BETTER A HUMBLE HOUSE THAN NONE. A MAN IS MASTER AT HOME. A PAIR OF GOATS AND A PATCHED ROOF ARE BETTER THAN BEGGING."

-THE HAVAMAL

THE GODS WILL ALWAYS SMILE ON THE BRAVE."

-VIKING PROVERB

EARLY VIKING PEOPLE
LIVED IN HOLLOWED OUT
HOLES IN HILLS WITH NO
WINDOWS, AND WOULD
USE ANIMAL EXCREMENT
TO FUEL FIRES.

WOMEN HAD RELATIVE FREEDOM COMPARED TO OTHER CULTURES. THEY COULD REMARRY AND DIVORCE, AND EVEN OWN PROPERTY.

IN SOME VIKING
SETTLEMENTS, THERE
WERE LAWS TO PROTECT
AGAINST THE
MISTREATMENT OR
DISHONORING A MAIDEN.
THESE "GOTLUND LAWS"
COULD RESULT IN HEAVY
FINES FOR THE
PERPETRATOR,
BANISHMENT, OR EVEN
BLOODSHED AND DEATH.

"I GREET THE SWORD'S HONED EDGE THAT BITES INTO MY FLESH, KNOWING THAT THIS COURAGE WAS GIVEN TO ME BY MY FATHER."

-GISLI

"HE WAS NURSED AND GREW ON THE SAP OF THE GROUND, ON THE ICE-COLD SEA AND THE SACRED BOAR'S BLOOD."

-CONCERNING HEIMDALL

GIRLS WERE MARRIED OFF TO FORM HOUSE ALLIANCES A YOUNG AS TWELVE YEARS OLD. THE GIRL HAD LET SAY IN THE MATTER AND WAS MORE OR LESS CONSIDERED PROPERTY OF THE FAMILY.

KITTENS WERE OFTEN GIVEN TO NEW BRIDES. THE KITTENS WERE A REPRESENTATIVE OF THE GODDESS FREYJA, WHO RODE IN A CART DRAWN BY CATS.

ARCHAEOLOGISTS HAVE DISCOVERED NUMEROUS GRAVES OF VIKING WOMEN BURIED WITH WEAPONS, SUGGESTING THAT WOMEN DID PERHAPS TAKE PART IN FIGHTING.

THE AVERAGE LIFE EXPECTANCY OF A VIKING WOMAN WAS AROUND 35 YEARS OF AGE. THIS IS DUE TO THE DANGERS OF CHILDBIRTH.

"VOLVA" WERE HONORED
AND WISE WOMEN. THEY
WERE CONSIDERED
HEALERS AND
PRIESTESSES. THE
VOLVA COULD TRAVEL
ALONE WITHOUT FEAR AND
WERE WELCOME BY ALL.

"THE MORE RENOWNED WOMAN OFTEN HAS FEWER RINGS."

-ICELANDIC PROVERB

IT WAS NOT UNHEARD OF
FOR FIRST BORN GIRLS TO
BE KILLED OR ABANDONED
IN HOPES OF A SON.

AS SOON AS A CHILD WAS ABLE, HE WOULD BE EXPECTED TO CONTRIBUTE TO THE FAMILY BY WORKING THE FARM, HUNTING LEARNING TO FIGHT, AND WORKING IN THE HOME. NORSE CHILDREN DID NOT GO TO SCHOOL.

"THE BURNT CHILD STAYS AWAY FROM THE FIRE."

IN THE EVENT OF A DIVORCE, HUSBANDS WOULD BE FORCED TO PAY MAINTENANCE TO THEIR EX-WIFE, SIMILAR TO ALIMONY AND CHILD SUPPORT WE HAVE TODAY.

IN HARSH WINTERS OR BAD
WEATHER, A VIKING
FAMILY WOULD BRING ALL
THEIR LIVESTOCK INTO
THEIR LIVING QUARTERS.

IF A VIKING WAS WEALTHY ENOUGH OR HAD ENOUGH FAMILY MEMBERS, THEY WOULD LIVE IN A "LONGHOUSE",

A MASSIVE WOODEN, SINGLE ROOMED HALL THAT WOULD HOUSE THE ENTIRE FAMILY FROM GRANDPARENTS TO GRANDCHILDREN.

A VIKING WHO FAILED TO PAY HIS TAXES OR FAILED TO SUPPORT HIS FAMILY THROUGH SUCCESSFUL CROPS, COULD BE FORCED INTO SLAVERY THROUGH POVERTY.

"ALL UNDONE IS NO ONE, THOUGH AT DEATH'S DOOR HE LIE. SOME WITH GOOD SONS ARE BLESSED, AND SOME WITH DEED WELL DONE."

-THE HAVAMAL

"DO WELL TO YOUR KINSMEN AND TAKE LITTLE REVENGE FOR THEIR WRONGDOINGS. ENDURE WITH PATIENCE AND YOU WILL WIN LONG-LASTING PRAISE."

-BRYNHILD

"A SON IS BETTER THOUGH LATE BEGOTTEN OF AN OLD AND AILING FATHER. ONLY YOUR KIN WILL PROUDLY CARVE A MEMORIAL AT THE MAIN GATE."

-THE HAVAMAL

HEIDRUN, IN NORSE MYTHOLOGY, IS THE NAME OF A GOAT WHO LIVES ON THE ROOF OF VALHALLA, FEEDING FROM THE BRANCHES OF THE WORLD TREE. FROM HER FOUR UDDERS COME WINE, MEAD, OLD BEER, AND RANGE BEER.

"DO NOT DISPUTE WITH THOSE WHO ARE DRUNK ON ALE AND HAVE LOST THEIR WITS."

-THE SAGA OF VOLSUNGS

VIKING LIVING QUARTERS DID NOT INCLUDE A BATHROOM OR PRIVY. THEY WOULD DO THEIR BUSINESS OUTSIDE AND CLEAN THEMSELVES WITH SHEEP'S WOOL, MOSS, OR SOMETHING SIMILAR.

A VIKING WAS CONSIDERED AN ADULT AT AGE 12 AND WOULD IMMEDIATELY TAKE ON RESPONSIBILITIES IN THEIR HOUSEHOLD.

VIKING DID NOT USE SILVERWARE OR EATING UTENSILS, AND ATE WITH THEIR MEALS ON THEIR LAPS AND USED THEIR FINGERS FOR ALL MEALS.

"A PALTRY MAN AND POOR
OF MIND AT ALL THINGS
EVER MARKS, FOR HE
NEVER KNOWS, WHAT HE
OUGHT TO KNOW, THAT HE
IS NOT FREE FROM
FAULTS."

"DO NOT SWEAR A HARD OATH, HARD VENGEANCE FOLLOWS THE BREAKING OF TRUCE."

-VOLSUNGA SAGA

IT IS SAID THAT VIKINGS WOULD OFTEN DOMESTICATE WILD ANIMALS TRAPPED AS CUBS, ESPECIALLY BEARS. BROWN BEARS WERE EVEN IMPORTED TO ICELAND WHERE THEY WERE KNOWN AS "HOUSE BEARS".

THE VIKINGS WERE ACTUALLY A VERY CLEAN PEOPLE AND TOOK GREAT CARE IN REGARDS TO THEIR HYGIENE. THEY TOOK COMBED AND WASHED THEIR HAIR AND BEARDS OFTEN, AND WERE ONE OF THE ONLY CULTURES TO REGULARLY TAKE BATHS AT THE TIME.

DUE TO THEIR IMPECCABLE HYGIENE AND FIERCENESS IN BATTLE, VIKING MEN WERE RENOWNED FOR THEIR ATTRACTIVENESS. IT WAS NOT UNCOMMON FOR WOMEN TO VOLUNTARILY BE TAKEN BY VIKINGS IN RAIDS.

THERE IS EVIDENCE OF VIKING TEETH BEING UNUSUALLY WORN AND WARPED DOWN. THIS IS MOST LIKELY DUE TO THE GRIT IN THE BREAD THEY ATE.

150

"WORK NOT DONE,

NEEDS NO REWARD."

"TOMORROW, SAYS THE LAZY."

-ICELANDIC PROVERB

"A MAN NEEDS WARMTH, THE WARMTH OF FIRE AND OF THE SHINING SUN. A HEALTHY MAN IS A HAPPY MAN WHO IS NEITHER ILL NOR INJURED."

-THE HAVAMAL

BLONDE HAIR WAS IDEAL
IN VIKING CULTURE, AND
MANY MEN WOULD DYE
THEIR HAIR AND BEARDS
BLONDE USING LYE SOAP.

CONTRARY TO POPULAR BELIEF, THERE IS NO HISTORICAL EVIDENCE OF VIKINGS EVER HAVING HORNS ON THEIR HELMETS.

"IT IS THE NORTH WIND THAT LASHES MEN INTO VIKINGS; IT IS SOFT, LUSCIOUS SOUTH WIND WHICH LULLS THEM TO LOTUS DREAMS."

-OUIDA

"THE NEWCOMER NEEDS FIRE, HIS KNEES ARE NUMB. A MAN WHO HAS MADE HIS WAY OVER THE MOUNTAINS NEEDS FOOD AND FRESH LINEN.

-THE HAVAMAL, ON HOSPITALITY

"IT IS FRIENDSHIP, WHEN A MAN CAN UTTER ALL HIS MIND TO ANOTHER."

OUTLAWS OR THOSE WHO
HAD COMMITTED SERIOUS
CRIMES HAD NO
PROTECTION FROM THE
LAW AND COULD BE
LEGALLY (AND
ENCOURAGINGLY) KILLED
BY ANYONE WITH NO
CONSEQUENCE.

A "THING" WAS THE
TERMED USED FOR A
GATHERING OF VIKING
MEN THAT'S PURPOSE WAS
TO DISCUSS THE LAW.

VIKINGS WOULD USE
"TESTS OF BRAVERY"
SOMETIMES TO SORT OUT A
DISPUTE. THESE COULD
INCLUDE BUT NOT LIMITED
TO: CARRYING HOT IRON
FOR TEN PACES OR PICKING
STONES OUT OF BOILING
WATER.

A LAWMAKER WOULD
ANNUALLY READ OUT ALL
OF SOCIETY'S LAWS IN A
PUBLIC PLACE, SO THAT
EVEN THE ILLITERATE MAY
KNOW, AND OBEY THE
LAWS.

"WHEN WE SPEAK MOST FAIRLY, WE THINK MOST FREELY."

-NORDIC PROVERB

"WHERE FAULT CAN BE FOUND, THE GOOD IS IGNORED."

-THE SAGA OF GRETTIR

THE VIKINGS EXPLORED
MOST OF THE NORTHERN
ATLANTIC, WEST TO NORTH
AMERICA, AS FAR SOUTH
AS NORTH AFRICA AND
EAST AS CONSTANTINOPLE
(MODERN ISTANBUL). SOME
ARCHAEOLOGICAL
EVIDENCE EVEN SUGGESTS
THEY WENT AS FAR EAST
AS BAGHDAD.

ONE OF THE BIGGEST ECONOMIC
REASONS FOR THE CONSTANT
VIKING RAIDS WAS THE TAKING
OF SLAVES THAT COULD BE SOLD
TO THE BOOMING EASTERN
SLAVE TRADE. THOUGH ONCE
CHRISTIANITY WAS TAKING ROOT
IN SCANDINAVIA, IT WAS
FROWNED UPON, IF NOT
OUTLAWED, TO SELL A FELLOW
CHRISTIAN INTO SLAVERY. THUS
BEING A MAJOR FACTOR IN THE
SHARP DECLINE OF RAIDS AND
SLAVE TAKING.

BESIDES THE SELLING OF SLAVES AND RAIDING, THE VIKINGS GAINED CONSIDERABLE WEALTH BY EXPORTING GOODS SUCH AS FURS, AMBER, CLOTH, WOOL, SALT A VARIETY OF MEATS, AND DOWN.

VIKINGS WERE
UNFAMILIAR WITH
COINAGE, AND USED A
BULLION ECONOMY,
MOSTLY CONSISTING OF
SILVER FASHIONED INTO
BARS.

"THOUGH GLAD AT HOME, AND MERRY WITH GUESTS, A MAN SHALL BE WARY AND WISE."

-THE HAVAMAL

YOU WILL REACH YOUR DESTINATION EVEN WHEN YOU TRAVEL SLOWLY."

"THE MAN WHO WALKS HIS OWN ROAD, WALKS ALONE."

-THE HAVAMAL

"NO BETTER BURDEN CAN A MAN CARRY ON THE ROAD THAN A STORE OF COMMON SENSE."

-THE HAVAMAL

AT MARKET, A VIKING BARTERING A CAPTURED SLAVE COULD EXPECT TO RECEIVE ABOUT 24 HEADS OF CATTLE IN EXCHANGE FOR A STRONG MAN, AND ABOUT 8 FOR A WOMAN.

GOOD TREATMENT OF SLAVES WAS NOT A SOCIETAL NORM TO VIKINGS. ALTHOUGH IN MOST CASES SLAVES WERE TREATED CRUELLY, SLAVES COULD WORK TOWARDS BUYING THEIR FREEDOM IF THEY WERE SKILLED ENOUGH.

"LET NONE PUT FAITH IN THE FIRST SOWN FRUIT."

-NORDIC PROVERB

"NOTHING VENTURED, NOTHING GAINED."

-THE SAGA OF NJAL

"THE MOST TRUSTED AND HELPING HAND IS AT THE END OF ONE'S OWN ARM."

"BECOME NOT A BEGGAR
TO THE MONEY YOU MAKE.
WHAT IS SAVED FOR A
FRIEND, A FOE MAY TAKE.
GOOD PLANS OFTEN GO
AWRY."

-THE HAVAMAL

IN 1000 A.D. CENTURIES
BEFORE CHRISTOPHER
COLUMBUS, THE NORSE
EXPLORER LEIF ERIKSSON
SAILED FROM GREENLAND
TO NORTH AMERICA,
EXPLORING AND SETTLING
THE LAND FOR A SHORT
TIME.

THE VIKINGS USED A CERTAIN FUNGUS CALLED "TOUCHWOOD" TO START FIRES. IT WAS MADE FROM THE BARK OF TREES BOILED IN URINE FOR SEVERAL DAYS. THE RESULT WAS A FELT-LIKE MATERIAL THAT WOULD SMOLDER RATHER THAN BURN. IT MADE AN EXCELLENT PORTABLE FIRE STARTER AND VIKINGS TRAVELLERS MADE MUCH USE OF IT.

IN THE EARLY 9TH CENTURY A
VIKING TRIBE FROM SWEDEN
CALLED THE "RUS" ENTERED
THE AREA OF WESTERN
MODERN RUSSIA. THEY
QUICKLY BECAME THE MORE
OR LESS "LEADERS" OF THE
NATIVE SLAVIC PEOPLES.
THESE RUS AND THEIR
DESCENDANTS ARE THOUGHT
TO HAVE BEEN WHERE
RUSSIA'S NAME ORIGINATES.

"NEVER BREAK THE PEACE WHICH TRUE AND GOOD MEN MAKE BETWEEN YOU AND OTHERS."

-THE SAGA OF NJAL

"HE THAT LEARNS NAUGHT
WILL NEVER KNOW HOW
ONE IS THE FOOL OF
ANOTHER, FOR IF ONE MAN
BE RICH ANOTHER IS POOR
AND FOR THAT SHOULD
BEAR NO BLAME."

"FEAR THE RECKONING OF THOSE YOU HAVE WRONGED."

THERE IS STRONG EVIDENCE THAT VIKINGS FARMED CANNABIS. ITS USES WERE MOSTLY LIKELY CEREMONIAL OR MEDICAL.

ERIK THE RED, WHOSE NICKNAME IS ATTRIBUTED TO HIS RED HAIR AND HOT TEMPER, AFTER BEING EXILED FROM ICELAND. SAILED WEST TO DISCOVER AN UNCHARTED ISLAND WHICH HE DUBBED "GREENLAND".

THE VIKINGS HAD SEVERAL DIFFERENT NAMES DEPENDING ON THE PEOPLES THEY INTERACTED WITH. TO THE GERMANS, THEY WERE THE ASHMEN, DUE TO THE ASH WOOD OF THEIR BOATS. TO THE GAELS, THEY WERE THE LAKEMEN, AND TO THE SAXONS THEY WERE KNOWN AS THE DENE.

THE BYZANTINES OFTEN REFERRED TO THE VIKINGS AS THE VARANGIANS, OR "SWORN MEN". THIS IS THOUGHT TO BE DUE TO THE BYZANTINE EMPERORS OFTEN EMPLOYING THEM AS PERSONAL BODYGUARDS, KNOWN MORE FAMOUSLY AS "THE VARANGIAN GUARD".

THERE ARE STORIES OF
CAMELS BEING BROUGHT
TO SCANDINAVIA FROM
VIKINGS WHO HAD
TRAVELED EAST. THOUGH
IT IS LIKELY NONE OF THE
BEASTS SURVIVED LONG
DUE TO THE CLIMATE.

"DECEIT SLEEPS WITH GREED."

"LOAD NO MAN WITH LAVISH GIFTS. SMALL PRESENTS OFTEN WIN GREAT PRAISE. WITH A LOAF OF BREAD AND A CUP SHARED, I FOUND FELLOWSHIP."

-THE HAVAMAL

"IT IS BETTER TO LIVE THAN LIE DEAD. A DEAD MAN GATHERS NO GOODS. I SAW WARM FIRE AT A WEALTHY MAN'S HOUSE HIMSELF DEAD AT THE DOOR."

-THE HAVAMAL

"NEVER IN SPEECH WITH A
FOOL, SHOULD YOU WASTE
A SINGLE WORLD."

MUSICIANSHIP WAS THE SIGN OF A CULTIVATED MAN IN VIKING CULTURE AND HIGHLY PRAISED. VIKINGS PLAYED AN ARRAY OF INSTRUMENTS INCLUDING LUTES, LYRES, FIDDLES, AND HARPS.

THE VIKINGS BELIEVED
THE THREE NORNS RULED
OVER FATE; PAST,
PRESENT, AND FUTURE.

"HE WILL WIN, WHO IS MOST STUBBORN."

"IT IS THE STILL AND SILENT SEA THAT DROWNS A MAN."

-THE HAVAMAL

"THE LAME RIDES A HORSE. THE MAIMED DRIVES THE HERD. THE DEAD IS BRAVE IN BATTLE. A MAN IS BETTER BLIND THAN BURIED. A DEAD MAN IS DEFT AT NOTHING."

-THE HAVAMAL

198

FOR ENTERTAINMENT, VIKINGS TOOK PART IN SPORTS, DICE GAMES, BOARD GAMES, AND MUSIC.

ALTHOUGH NOT CERTAIN,
SOME SCHOLARS BELIEVE
AN EARLY VERSION OF
CHESS WAS INVENTED BY
THE NORSE, WHO CARVED
THE PIECES OUT OF
WALRUS TUSK.

SPORTS AND OTHER ATHLETIC ACTIVITIES, WERE HIGHLY REGARDED IN NORSE CULTURE. THE MOST POPULAR SPORTS INCLUDE WRESTLING, FIST BOXING, SPEAR AND STONE THROWING, STONE LIFTING, MOUNTAIN CLIMBING, AND SWIMMING.

BLOOD SPORTS IN PARTICULAR WERE POPULAR IN NORSE CULTURE INCLUDING BEAR BAITING, HORSE FIGHTING, DOG FIGHTING AND COCK FIGHTING.

"PUSH AWAY YOUR PRIDE! YOUR STRENGTH, YOUR POWER, ARE YOURS FOR HOW MANY YEARS? DEATH COMETH FASTER THAN YOU THINK AND NONE CAN FLEE IT."

-BEOWULF

"THE BLOOD SOAKED CLUB ALWAYS FINDS ITS MARK."

-NORDIC PROVERB

THERE ARE ACCOUNTS OF
A SPECIAL ACTIVITY
VIKING MEN WOULD TAKE
PART IN, MORE OR LESS
FOR BRAGGING RIGHTS. IT
WAS CALLED "OAR
JUMPING", WHICH
INVOLVED A MAN JUMPING
FROM OAR TO OAR ON A
SHIP WHILST IT WAS
ROWING.

VIKING LONGSHIPS WERE INCREDIBLY SWIFT FOR THEIR TIME. A LONGSHIP COULD ON AVERAGE TRAVEL UP TO 200 KILOMETERS A DAY.

VIKING LONGSHIPS WERE EQUIPPED WITH SAILS AND OARS, AND WERE STEERED BY A STEERING OAR AT THE BACK OF THE BOAT. LONGSHIPS WERE ABOUT 30 METERS IN LENGTH AND COULD CARRY UP TO 60 MEN.

"OVER THE FOAMING SALT SEA SPRAY THE NORSE SEA-HORSES TOOK THEIR WAY, RACING ACROSS THE OCEAN-PLAIN."

-HEIMSKRINGLA

"THE BOLD VIKINGS LOST MANY A MAN OF THEIR HOST, EIGHT GALLEYS TO WITH CARGO AND CREW."

-HEIMSKRINGLA

"WHEN NEED BEFALLS ME TO SAVE MY VESSEL, I HUSH THE WIND ON THE STORMY WAVE AND SOOTHE ALL THE SEA TO REST."

-WORDS OF ODIN

VIKINGS WOULD USE
WHALE AND SEAL SKIN TO
MAKE STRONG ROPE FOR
THEIR LONGSHIPS.

VIKINGS WOULD CARVE
FRIGHTENING
FIGUREHEADS OF
MONSTERS ONTO THEIR
LONGSHIP PROWS, AS A
MEANS TO TERRIFY THEIR
ENEMIES.

"THE TRAVELLER MUST TRAIN HIS WITS. ALL IS EASY AT HOME. HE WHO KNOWS LITTLE IS A LAUGHING STOCK AMONGST THE MEN OF THE WORLD."

-THE HAVAMAL

"A BAD ROWER BLAMES THE OAR."

-ICELANDIC PROVERB

THE TERRIFYING
FIGUREHEADS CARVED ON
THE FRONT OF VIKING
LONGSHIPS WERE NOT
ONLY MEANT TO SCARE
ENEMIES, BUT ALSO TO
DRIVE SEA MONSTERS AND
OTHER MYTHICAL SEA
CREATURES AWAY.

VIKINGS WOULD REMOVE
THE FRIGHTENING
FIGUREHEADS ON THEIR
LONGSHIP PROWS WHILST
IN FRIENDLY WATERS AS
TO NOT OFFEND THE GODS.

"THERE SELDOM IS A SINGLE WAVE."

"THE BROTHERLESS MAN'S BACK IS ALWAYS VULNERABLE."

-THE SAGA OF GRETTIR

"THE HEAD ONLY KNOWS WHAT LIES NEAREST TO THE HEART."

AT SEA, THE VIKINGS WOULD KEEP AND USE HALF-STARVED RAVENS TO HELP THEM FIND LAND, BEING THAT, AS SOON AS LET LOOSE, A STARVING RAVEN WOULD IMMEDIATELY HEAD TOWARDS LAND.

IN SEA BATTLES, THE VIKINGS MAIN OBJECTIVE WAS TO CAPTURE ENEMY SHIPS, NOT DESTROY THEM. THIS WAS DUE TO THE FACT THAT THE VIKINGS MAIN OBJECTIVE WAS ALWAYS LOOTING AND ECONOMIC GAIN.

"IT IS BEST TO SEARCH WHILE THE TRAIL IS NEW."

"I SAW AND WAS SILENT. I SAW AND I PONDERED. I LISTENED TO THE SPEECH OF MEN."

"THE WOLF AND THE DOG DO NOT PLAY TOGETHER."

-ANCIENT NORSE PROVERB

"TO BE WITHOUT SILVER IS BETTER THAN TO BE WITHOUT HONOR."

-NORDIC PROVERB

HAFGUFA IS A LEGENDARY SEA MONSTER IN NORSE MYTHOLOGY. HE IS SAID TO DISGUISE HIMSELF AS ENTIRE ISLANDS OR ROCKS RISING FROM THE SEA.

LYNGBAKR IS A MASSIVE WHALE-LIKE CREATURE IN NORSE MYTHOLOGY. LYNGBAKR DISGUISES HIMSELF AS ISLANDS IN THE SEA AND WHEN A SHIP CREW LANDED ON HIM, HE WOULD DIVE INTO THE SEA, DROWNING THE CREW.

"BE NEVER THE FIRST WITH FRIEND OF THINE TO BREAK THE BOND OF FELLOWSHIP."

"A MAN SHOULD KNOW HOW MANY LOG STUBS AND STRIPS OF BARK TO COLLECT IN THE SUMMER TO KEEP IN STOCK WOOD FOR HIS WINTER FIRES."

-THE HAVAMAL

THE TRADITIONAL VIKING GREETING IS SAID "EY UP".

MOST MODERN WORDS WITH THE "SK" SOUND HAIL FROM THE NORSE TONGUE, SUCH AS SKILL, SKIRT, SKULL, SKIN, SCATTER AND SCAB.

"UNMANLY ONE, CEASE, OR MY MIGHTY HAMMER, MJOLNIR, WILL CLOSE THY MOUTH."

-THOR TO LOKI, LOKASENNA

232

"BETTER ALONE THAN IN BAD COMPANY"

-NORDIC PROVERB

THE MOST LIKELY REASON AS TO WHY THE VIKING RAIDS WERE SO SUCCESSFUL WAS THE FACT THAT AT THE TIME, ENGLAND AND OTHER PARTS OF EUROPE, LACKED ANY REAL NAVAL FORCES TO MEET THE VIKINGS ON WATER.

THE LACK OF A UNIFICATION ENGLAND IN THE EARLY VIKING AGE MEANT TOWNS MORE OR LESS FENDED FOR THEMSELVES. THIS DISUNITY RESULTED IN EASY PREY FOR VIKING RAIDERS, WHO COULD PICK OFF TOWNS AND VILLAGES ONE BY ONE.

AFTER CENTURIES OF CONFLICT, A VIKING KING SAT ON THE ENGLISH THRONE. HIS NAME WAS KING CNUT.

"WHEN YOU RECOGNISE EVIL, SPEAK OUT AGAINST IT, AND GIVE NO TRUCE TO YOUR ENEMY."

"OFTEN IN THE WOODS, IS A LISTENER NIGH."

-THE SAGA OF GRETTIR

"TWO WOODEN STAKES STOOD IN THE FIELD; THERE I HUNG MY HAT AND CLOAK. THEY HAD CHARACTER IN FINE CLOTHES. NOW NAKED, I WAS NOTHING."

-THE HAVAMAL

"SPEAK USEFUL WORDS OR BE SILENT."

-THE HAVAMAL

IT HAS BEEN RECORDED THAT THE VERY SIGHT OF A VIKING LONGSHIP ON THE HORIZON WOULD CAUSE ENTIRE VILLAGES TO BE ABANDONED, THE INHABITANTS FLEEING WITH THEIR VALUABLES AND LIVESTOCK.

A FLEET OF MORE THAN 350 LONGSHIPS ATTACKED THE CITY OF LONDON VIA THE RIVER THAMES IN 851 A.D.

"ONE SHOULD LISTEN WHEN AN OLD DOG BARKS."

"IT IS FORTUNATE TO BE FAVOURED WITH PRAISE AND POPULARITY. IT IS DIRE LUCK TO BE DEPENDENT ON THE FEELING OF FELLOW-MAN."

-THE HAVAMAL

A MAJOR POINT IN THE
SUCCESS OF VIKINGS IN
BATTLE WAS THEIR
COMPLETE IGNORANCE OF
STANDARD EUROPEAN
"RULES OF WAR". THEY
RELIED ON STEALTH,
DECEIT, AVOID PITCHED
BATTLES, AND WOULD
FIGHT ANYWHERE, EVEN
ON HOLY SITES. TO THE
VIKINGS NONE OF THESE
VIRTUES WERE SEEN AS

COWARDLY, MERELY AN EASY RECIPES FOR VICTORY.

IN BATTLE, VIKINGS WERE KNOWN TO HAVE FORMED A WEDGE FORMATION. WITH THEIR TOUGHEST AND STRONGEST WARRIORS IN THE FRONT, THEY WOULD ATTEMPT TO SMASH THROUGH AN ENEMY FORMATION WHERE THEY COULD THEN FIGHT IN SINGLE COMBAT.

"FOR HEROES, TIS' SEEMLY THE TRUTH TO SPEAK."

-HELGAKVIOA HUNDINGSBANA II

"GREAT GLORY WE HAVE GAINED, THOUGH NOW OR TOMORROW WE WILL DIE. NO ONE LIVES TIL EVE AGAINST THE NORNS' DECREE."

"AS FOR ME, PEOPLE WILL BE PLEASED TO ESCAPE FROM ME STILL IN ONE PIECE."

-GRETTIR, SAGA OF GRETTIR THE STRONG

IN LATER TIMES, THE
VIKING'S AXE WAS
MODIFIED WITH A LONGER,
CURVED BLADE,
ALLOWING HIM TO "HOOK"
AN OPPONENT'S LEG AND
OFF SET HIM.

VIKING SAGAS INDICATE THAT CARRYING A RED SHIELD MEANT VIOLENT INTENT.

PROMINENT VIKINGS SUCH AS JARLS OR GREAT WARRIORS, UPON DEATH, WERE LAID TO REST IN BOATS. THEIR CORPSE WOULD BE SURROUNDED BY ANYTHING THEY THOUGHT WOULD HELP THEM REACH THEIR FINAL DESTINATION. THIS INCLUDED WEAPONS, FINE GOODS, AND EVEN SACRIFICED SLAVES.

"BRAWL WITH A PIG AND YOU LEAVE WITH HIS STINK."

"A WISE MAN'S HEART IS SELDOM CHEERFUL."

-OLD NORDIC PROVERB

ONION SOUP WAS ADMINISTERED TO THE WOUNDED AND SICK. THE SEVERITY OF THE WOUND WOULD DEPEND ON WHETHER OR NOT ONE COULD SMELL AN ONION ODOR COMING FROM THE WOUND A FEW HOURS AFTER BEING DRANK.

HUNDREDS OF TOMBSTONES HAVE BEEN DISCOVERED WITH CARVINGS OF PERSONAL ACHIEVEMENTS OR DEEDS. BRAGGING WAS AN IMPORTANT VIRTUE IN NORSE SOCIETY.

TEMPLES WERE VERY UNCOMMON IN VIKING CULTURE. INSTEAD, NORSE FOLK WOULD CHOOSE CERTAIN LANDMARKS FOR PLACES OF WORSHIP SUCH AS WATERFALLS, STRANGE TREES, AND ODDLY SHAPED ROCKS.

"ASK YOU MUST AND ANSWER WELL TO BE CALLED CLEVER. ONE MAY KNOW YOUR SECRET, NEVER A SECOND. IF THREE KNOW, THREE THOUSAND SOON AFTER."

-THE HAVAMAL

"HAPPY IS HE WHO HATH IN HIMSELF PRAISE AND WISDOM IN LIFE."

-NORDIC PROVERB

259

"BARKING DOGS SELDOM BITE."

THE NORMANS WERE
DESCENDED FROM THE
VIKINGS. A GROUP OF
VIKINGS WERE GIVEN
FEUDAL OWNERSHIP OF
THE AREA OF NORTHERN
FRANCE IN THE 10TH
CENTURY, KNOWN THEN AS
THE DUCHY OF
NORMANDY. IN THE
AGREEMENT, THEY WOULD
CONVERT TO
CHRISTIANITY AND

DEFEND THE LAND AGAINST THEIR OWN PEOPLE, WHO OFTEN RAIDED THE NORTHERN COAST OF FRANCE.

WILLIAM THE CONQUEROR WAS THE GRANDSON OF THE VIKING KING ROLLO.

CATHOLIC CHURCH
LEADERS BELIEVED THE
VIKINGS HAD BEEN SENT
BY GOD AS PUNISHMENT
FOR ITS PEOPLE'S SINS.

"SPEAK TO THE POINT, OR BE STILL."

-THE HAVAMAL

264

"AS THE OLD BIRD SINGS, SO DOES THE YOUNG BIRD TWEET."

"HIS HANDS ARE CLEAN WHO WARMS ANOTHER."

-THE SAGA OF NJAL

NEAR THE END OF THE VIKING AGE, VIKING RAIDS BECAME MUCH LESS FREQUENT AND PROFITABLE. ALSO, BY THIS TIME MOST EUROPEAN LANDS NOW HAD FORTIFIED DEFENSES AND TRAINED ARMIES TO SUCCESSFULLY DEFEND AGAINST SUCH RAIDS.

NEAR THE END OF THE AGE, THE VIKINGS AS A WHOLE WERE BEGINNING TO LOSE THEIR IDENTITY. THEY WERE NO LONGER REFERRED TO AS "VIKINGS" OR "NORSEMEN", BUT WOULD BEGIN TO IDENTIFY AS SWEDES, NORWEGIANS, DANES, ETC.

"BOLD VIKINGS, NOT SLOW.
TO THE DEATH FRAY TO
GO, MEET OUR NOSE KING
BY CHANCE, AND THEIR
GALLEYS ADVANCE."

-HEIMSKRINGLA

"HE UTTERS TOO MANY FUTILE WORDS WHO IS NEVER SILENT. A GARRULOUS TONGUE, IF NOT CHECKED, SINGS OFTEN TO ITS OWN HARM."

-THE HAVAMAL

BY THE END OF THE VIKING AGE, AROUND THE 11TH CENTURY, THE CATHOLIC CHURCH WAS GAINING MORE INFLUENCE IN SCANDINAVIA. PAGANISM WAS ON THE DECLINE AND UNIFIED CATHOLIC NATIONS WERE BEGINNING TO TAKE SHAPE, SUCH AS THE KINGDOMS OF SWEDEN, NORWAY, AND DENMARK.

WHEN CHRISTIANITY
SPREAD THROUGHOUT
SCANDINAVIA, IT WAS
BELIEVED THAT BUILDING
ROADS AND BRIDGES
HELPED YOUR SOUL GO TO
HEAVEN.

THE VIKING AGE IS SAID TO HAVE ENDED IN 1066 A.D FOLLOWING THEIR DEFEAT AT THE BATTLE OF STAMFORD BRIDGE, WHERE THE NORWEGIAN KING HARALDR WAS KILLED.

"A BAD FRIEND IS FAR AWAY THOUGH HIS COTTAGE IS CLOSE. A TRUE FRIEND LIES A TRODDEN ROAD THOUGH HIS FARM LIES FAR AWAY."

-THE HAVAMAL

274

"OLD FRIENDS ARE THE LAST TO BREAK AWAY."

-THE SAGA OF GRETTIR

"CLOSER THE ARMY CAME,
THE GREATER IT GREW,
THEIR WEAPONS
SPARKLING LIKE A FIELD
OF BROKEN ICE."

-KING HARALD'S SAGA

THE OLDEST TREE ON A FARM OR PLOT OF LAND WAS CONSIDERED A "WARDEN TREE". THE BREAKING OF A SINGLE BRANCH OR TWIG ON THE TREE WAS CONSIDERED A SERIOUS OFFENCE.

THE NORSE BELIEVED WIGHTS LIVED UNDER THE ROOTS OF WARDEN TREES. THEY WOULD LEAVE TREATS AT THE TREE'S BASE AS A MEANS TO APPEASE THE SPIRITS AND BRING GOOD FORTUNE.

278

"AS MANY LIMBS WE HAVE CLEAVED, SHIELDS WE HAVE SPLIT, HELMETS AND CHIEFTAINS WE HAVE CUT DOWN, THE ENCOUNTERS WITH THE DEAD ARE THE GRIMMEST."

"ALL DEAD MEN'S GHOSTS GROW MORE DREADFUL AS DAYLIGHT DARKENS TO THE DIMNESS OF NIGHT."

-HELGAKVIO HUNDINGSBANA

"IN FRONT OF THE DOORS
OF VALHALLA IN ASGARD
IS A GROVE CALLED
GLASIR, WHOSE FOLIAGE
CONSISTS ENTIRELY OF
RED GOLD."

ODIN IS CALLED FATHER OF
THE SLAIN BECAUSE ALL
THOSE THAT FALL IN
BATTLE WERE HIS
ADOPTED SONS.

TWO RAVENS SIT ON
ODIN'S SHOULDERS, AND
INTO HIS EARS THEY
WHISPER ALL THE NEWS
THEY SEE OR HEAR.

THEIR NAMES ARE HUGIN
AND MUNIN.

"TO ODIN MANY A SOUL WAS DRIVEN. TO ODIN MANY A RICH GIFT GIVEN. LOUD RAGED THE STORM ON THE BATTLEFIELD. AXE RANG ON HELM AND SWORD ON SHIELD."

"ODIN'S MEN RUSHED FORWARD WITHOUT ARMOR, AS MAD AS DOGS OR WOLVES, BIT THEIR SHIELDS AND WERE AS STRONG AS BEARS."

"TO HEROES ODIN WILL SUPPLY, STRENGTH TO VANQUISH OR TO DIE."

-VOLUSPA HIM SKAMMA

"WHEN THE WATCHMAN OF THE GODS SHALL BLOW THE SHRIEKING HORN, THE WARRIOR SONS OF ODIN WILL BE SUMMONED TO THE FINAL BATTLE."

THUNDER AND LIGHTNING
WAS BELIEVED TO BE
CREATED BY THOR
WIELDING HIS MIGHTY
HAMMER, "MJOLNIR"

THE LANDVAETTIR, IN
NORSE MYTHOLOGY, ARE
THE SPIRITS OF THE ENTIRE
LAND. THEY ARE THE
GUARDIANS OF SPECIFIC
PLACES, WHETHER THAT
PLACE BE A ROCK, TREE,
TOWN, OR COUNTRY.

"HAMINGJA" IS THE OLD
NORSE TERM ASSOCIATED
WITH LUCK OR GOOD
FORTUNE.

"SEEK NEVER TO DRAW THYSELF INTO LOVE-WHISPERING WITH ANOTHER'S WIFE."

-NORDIC PROVERB

"IT IS NOT FATED THAT WE SHOULD LIVE TOGETHER. I AM A SHIELD-MAIDEN. I WEAR A HELMET AND RIDE TO WAR WITH WARRIOR KINGS."

-BRYNHILD

RATATOSKR IS THE SQUIRREL WHO RUNS UP AND DOWN THE WORLD TREE, YGGDRASIL. HE CARRIES MESSAGES BETWEEN THE DRAGON NIDHOGG AND THE HAWK VEORFOLNIR.

GARMER IN NORSE MYTHOLOGY IS SAID TO BE A BLOODSOAKED DOG OR WOLF. HE IS THE GUARDIAN OF HEL'S GATE. GARMER IS VERY AKIN TO CERBERUS IN GREEK MYTHOLOGY, THOUGH LACKING THE THREE HEADS.

IN NORSE MYTHOLOGY THE
MARNENNILL AND
MARGYGUR WERE MERMEN
(HALF MAN HALF FISH)
WHO COULD PROPHESIZE
THE FUTURE.

"IT IS RARE TO FIND ONE TO TRUST AMONGST MEN WHO DWELL BENEATH ODIN'S GALLOWS, FOR THE DARK MINDED SWAP BROTHER FOR TREASURE."

-THE SAGA OF EGIL

A LYING TONGUE CAN BEREFT HIM OF LIFE, AND ALL WITHOUT REASON OF RIGHT."

HOARDS OF COINS AND TREASURE ARE STILL BEING DISCOVERED IN ENGLAND FROM THE TIME OF THE GREAT VIKING RAID IN 865 A.D. THE ENGLISH WERE SO TERRIFIED THEY BURIED ALL THEIR WEALTH BEFORE FLEEING FROM THEIR COASTAL TOWNS. IT SEEMS THEY DID NOT RETURN FOR IT.

"VOROR" IN NORSE MYTHOLOGY IS THE SPIRIT WHICH FOLLOWS A PERSON THROUGHOUT LIFE, FROM BIRTH TO DEATH. IT IS SIMILAR TO A "GUARDIAN SPIRIT" OR A SORT OF CONSCIENCE.

THE PEOPLE OF ANCIENT SCANDINAVIA WERE THOUGHT TO HAVE INVENTED THE SPORT OF SKIING. SKIS WERE MAINLY USED AS A WAY TO GET AROUND BUT ALSO FOR FUN.

THEY EVEN HAD A GOD, ULLR, WHO WAS ASSOCIATED WITH SKIING.

L'ANSE AUX MEADOWS IS A NATIONAL HISTORICAL SITE IN NEWFOUNDLAND, CANADA. IT INCLUDES THE REMAINS OF AN 11TH CENTURY VIKING SETTLEMENT AND IS THE ONLY KNOWN AUTHENTIC EVIDENCE OF NORSE SETTLEMENT IN NORTH AMERICA.

THE END

58564101R00170

Made in the USA
Lexington, KY
13 December 2016